Expecting Your First Baby

First Pregnancy Ultimate Guide

By Cathy Wilson

Copyright © 2014

Income Disclaimer

This book contains business strategies, marketing methods and other business advice that, regardless of my own results and experience, may not produce the same results (or any results) for you. I make absolutely no guarantee, expressed or implied, that by following the advice below you will make any money or improve current profits, as there are several factors and variables that come into play regarding any given business.

Primarily, results will depend on the nature of the product or business model, the conditions of the marketplace, the experience of the individual, and situations and elements that are beyond your control.
As with any business endeavor, you assume all risk related to investment and money based on your own discretion and at your own potential expense.

Liability Disclaimer
By reading this book, you assume all risks associated with using the advice given below, with a full understanding that you, solely, are responsible for anything that may occur as a result of putting this information into action in any way, and regardless of your interpretation of the advice.
You further agree that our company cannot be held responsible in any way for the success or failure of your business as a result of the information presented in this book. It is your responsibility to conduct your own due diligence regarding the safe and successful operation of your business if you intend to apply any of our information in any way to your business operations.

Terms of Use

Expecting Your First Baby

First Pregnancy Ultimate Guide

By Cathy Wilson

Table of Contents

Introduction

Having a baby is an exciting time in a couple's life. Full of emotions, both high and low, worries and fears, moments of indecision, and yes, even a little panic. No worries - it's normal.

If this is your first baby, you might as well get used to the fact you're in unchartered territory, and just aren't going to *know until you know!*

Your body's going to go through all sorts of scary and absolutely fantabulous changes that defy all odds. To think that your cervix, which is about the size of a small coin, will expand to **TEN CENTIMETERS** in diameter, in order to give birth, seems absolutely crazy! But that's the reality in order for a baby to be delivered naturally.

Comforting Fact - *Welcome Baby Home* neonatal specialists, report babies react to stimuli from external sources while kicking, punching, frowning, and squirming, within their comforting warm-fluid filled womb. This means both mom and dad can read stories, rub and pat the tummy, and tell your unborn child about your day, and bond even before birth!

You need to use these nine months or so, to gather information and prepare for your little miracle's debut. Keep your mind open, and understand your plans may change by choice, or for unforeseen medical reasons.

Try to take it all in stride, because the most important factors here, are that your new baby is born healthy, and that you go through the birth process as smooth and comfortable as possible.

Let's get started!

The Science behind Conception

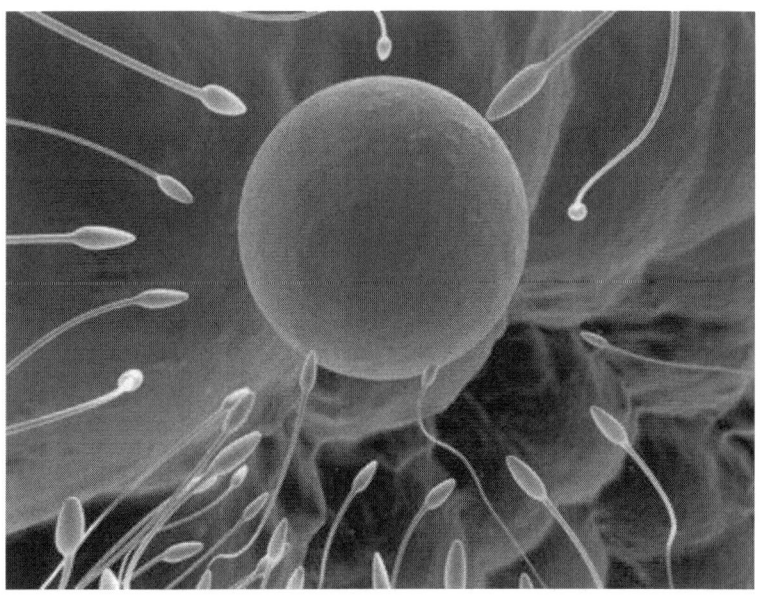

Some couples have no trouble conceiving. They don't have to worry about timing, basil temperature, ovulation predictor kits, or checking the consistency of vaginal secretions, in order to make conception happen. Nor do they have to get into fertility treatments, which are very stressful and often disappointing.

In order to make a baby, you need an ideal fertile environment, an egg that's ripe, and sperm that's viable. The egg meets the sperm in the Fallopian tube, after swimming strongly through your fertile egg-white cervical mucus, in search of the perfect ovum or egg.

Ovum - A female reproductive cell which, after fertilization, transforms into a zygote that soon develops into a baby, according to *Dr. J. Shaugnhessy, PhD.*

A typical menstrual cycle lasts 28 days, where on the 14th day an egg is released that starts to make its way down the Fallopian tubes in search of a sperm to fertilize it. This fertilization usually occurs 7-10 days after the egg is released. That's how long it usually takes to trek down to the uterus.

If the egg isn't fertilized, menstruation occurs.

If it's fertilized successfully, the egg implants in the uterus wall, and starts growing and dividing. Often when the egg implants, it causes implantation bleeding. This is just a little bit of bloody discharge that occurs a few days before the expected period. Not enough to fill a pad, but usually enough to notice. Some women use this as a very early symptom of pregnancy.

That's the very basics of the conception process. The best thing you can do here is to try and relax.

My Thoughts . . .

As I mentioned earlier, sometimes conception seems almost effortlessly. Other times it takes months, or even years to happen. Try to use this time to get your body and mind ready for pregnancy, and keep stress away as much as possible.

You'd be surprised how much anxiety and worry puts a damper on trying to conceive a baby, both physically and mentally.

And when all else fails, just keep trying, and trying again.

Believe *it and it* ***WILL*** *happen!*

Tips for Planning Conception

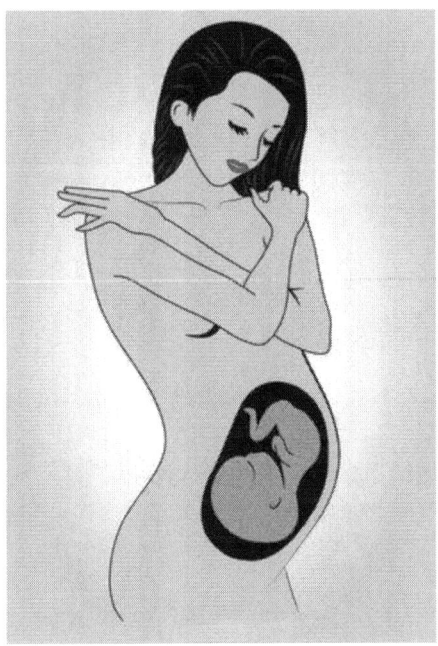

Contrary to what you may believe, the stork isn't always ready to deliver first time around. In order to get pregnant, skills are required, and timing is critical.

Some people just don't bother with timed intercourse, and take to having coitus every other day until they see the stick turn pink or blue. Let me tell you right now, that can quickly turn into an exhausting plan that'll forever sway your thoughts on sex for both of you, and not for the better.

A smarter strategy is to relax, and just wing it initially. Have sex when you're in the mood to keep it spontaneous and exciting. If you haven't hit the jackpot after the first few months, pay closer attention to your most fertile times.

Without getting too technical, there's about a week at best where you're most fertile in your monthly cycle. It makes sense this is the time to ensure you've got plenty of *viable* sperm swimming around in your uterus, shortly before, and a few days after this window of opportunity.

You just want to make sure you cover don't miss your change to get pregnant!

FACT - Not every woman ovulates on day 14 of her cycle. That's a gynormous misconception.
In fact, most *normal* healthy women don't ovulate on day 14. It's just the easiest way for experts to explain the whole concept of conception universally.

Some women release an egg as early as day 11, or as late as day 25. If you ovulate before day 11, you're not likely to get pregnant, because the egg simply hasn't had enough time to develop for proper growth.

So how do you know when you ovulate?

Count your first day of bleeding as day one, and on your next cycle, the first day of bleeding is day one. So, the difference between the two is your cycle length.

Now count back 14-16 days from the first day of your next period, and that will be *approximately* when you've ovulated. Although it could be a day or two earlier or later.

The week around this window is your most fertile time. It's when your cervical mucus is clear, abundant and stretchy, it's less acidic too and favorable for a few sperm swimmers.

Many women report the mucus discharge similar to egg whites. Disgusting, but bang on accurate!

Learning how your cycle works is the first step to successfully creating your little miracle.

Here are a few more pointers that will help you make it happen.

*Get a pre-baby checkup

It's important that both you and your partner are healthy, and all your parts are working before you start trying to have a baby. This will alleviate a whole load of frustrations if you have trouble conceiving.

If you find issues off the top, at least you're able to look at your options, and deal with them a.s.a.p.!

Also make sure you take a prenatal vitamin that has folic acid prior to conceiving. This ensures you're getting all the vitamins and minerals your baby needs to grow, and it helps prevent serious birth defects.

Prevention is the key, so go and get your checkups, both of you!

*Learn about your cycle

As I mentioned previously, it's important to get to know your cycle. The more you know about your cycle, the better.

Information is knowledge, and knowledge is power.

If you know when you ovulate, you'll increase the chances of hitting the bull's eye quickly.

*Never mind the wives-tales about positioning

The best advice for sexual positioning, is whatever makes you most comfortable. If you have a favorite position, you're just as likely to get you pregnant as any other. The only ones that may not pose favorable are standing up and the woman on top.

Simply because the sperm has to work harder to swim up towards the Fallopian tubes. Don't make the swimmers swim uphill if you don't have to!

Gravity is your friend!

*Chill after sex

Relax after you've just had a wild round of *conception trying* sex. Don't jump out of bed and head to the shower right away. This encourage those poor swimmers to literally drain away.

Experts from *WebMD*, suggest placing a pillow under your butt, raising your hips up a tad. Elevating them makes the trek much easier for those hard working swimmers. It helps you psychosomatically anyway.

Do this for about 15 minutes after sex, then go about your day with a positive mind, and a smile upon your beautiful face.

*Don't overdo it

This refers to life in general. Research studies show, a relaxed and positive attitude significantly increases your chances of conceiving a baby successfully. So relax in the stress department. Make the time to take a warm bath and relax before bed, or get your nails done. And definitely make sure you schedule *me time* every day.

It won't be long before you have a little one to take care of, and *me time* will be extinct!

*Lose weight and get healthy

This one's important. If you aren't feeling good about yourself now, you're not going to feel good about yourself during, or after the pregnancy. Shen all your hormones are going crazy, and you're carrying around extra baby weight.

Make sure your weight is in the healthy range for you, and pay close attention to your eating. Be sure you're getting all the healthy nutrients your body needs before you get pregnant. And if you don't exercise regularly already, make sure you get yourself set up on a program with a qualified trainer to start.

Keeping your weight in check by exercising and eating right, helps pave a smooth path in pregnancy. Research also shows this encourages an *easier* delivery. It's important you're healthy for your baby; mind, body, and *attitude*.

According to *Penn State University* researchers, overweight women, or women with the mentality of eating for two, were more likely to gain excessive amounts of weight during pregnancy.

And if you are extremely overweight, you may want to hold off on trying to have a baby until you've got your weight closer to the healthy range for you.

Nine months of having your body over is a long time. It's very stressful and tough on your body and mind. Having extra weight doesn't make it easier.

Studies also show, regular exercise helps to keep the weight gain under control. This varies from woman to woman, but's usually around the 20-30 pound range for one baby.

If you're having twins or triplets, it may be 35-45, and 45-55 pounds respectively. Your doctor will guide and direct you.

*Take a vacation

I kid you not! Many couples have found by taking a step away of their never-ending stressful lives, and vacation-ing, they conceive! The theory behind this, is stress and anxiety is hugely interconnected with your body's ability to get pregnant.

Alleviate the stress, relax the mind, and voila - a baby is conceived!

*Don't quit

Quitters never win here. If you want to truly have a baby you're going to have to be persistent and patient. It may happen right away, or it may take a sometime. Try not to pressure yourself, and enjoy the process. It'll happen when it's supposed to, so just go with that.

My Thoughts . . .

Sex is fun right? My advice to you, is try and keep it that way when attempting to conceive a baby. Don't stress, relax, and enjoy the ride, *rather than get all caught up in it, which I know is tough to do.*

Stay positive and use the pointers above, and you'll hit the nail on the head when the time's right.

Am I Pregnant? (Symptoms, Signs and Signals, and Testing)

I know you've likely heard of women that knew they were pregnant from the night of conception. Okay - but that's still *after-the-fact,* right? In other words, women that *knew* they were pregnant before they could actually test to verify, were just speculating.

FACT - There are early pregnancy tests that claim to verify pregnancy up to 5 days before your expected period. What you need to understand, is there are always exceptions to the rules.

FACT - The earlier you test, the increased chance the test is wrong. Or that you *were* indeed pregnant, but had a very early miscarriage.

American Pregnancy reports miscarriage is a threatened complication, or pregnancy loss under 20 weeks.

The *American College of Obstetricians and Gynecologists* research shows, up to 25% of all clinical recognized pregnancies end in miscarriage.

Without these early tests, most women wouldn't have even known they were pregnant. Something to consider, because it can be heartbreaking to test early.

Most experts agree, you should wait to test until a few days after you expect your period. This way, if you miscalculated by a few days, you aren't likely to get inaccurate results.

Hold yourself back and wait at least 2-3 weeks after you think you conceived, to do your testing.

Here are a few VERY EARLY signs that COULD point to pregnancy:

*Cramps

You've gotta know your cycle and your body for this one. When the embryo implants into your uterus, some women report *slight* cramping, along with some slight reddish-brownish discharge. Just enough to make you aware and wonder, if baby-making is on your mind.

It will seem a little odd, and could very well be an early pregnancy sign.

*Tender Breasts

This is a common one. All of a sudden your breast get incredibly tender to touch, so much so, they'll actually hurt. This is an exciting, yet painful moment for many. It makes sense, because your hormones are working over-time, and blood flow to your breasts is increased zippy fast.

*Extreme Unusual Tiredness

You've gotta be extremely honest with yourself here. Cuz there are just too many other factors besides pregnancy that could leave you suddenly tired. So use common sense and don't jump the gun.

What might happen, is you'll suddenly feel extremely tired. A feeling you can't recall ever having before. If it starts about the week before your period is due, you might figure out in a few weeks, it was your body signaling to you that you've conceived!

It's best to chalk these early signs as clues. The more clues you have, the better the chances your suspicions are correct.

*Nausea

This really is a common pregnancy symptom, and rightly so, with the increased demands on your bodily systems. Not to mention the huge doses of extra hormones.

The *British Medical Journal,* reports a whopping 70-85% of women experience nausea in their first trimester.

There are many women that begin feeling queasy well before their period is expected. Don't get too excited though, because the *morning sickness* stuff doesn't kick in until around the 6th week of pregnancy.

*Bloating

Ah, that lovely *whale* feeling that seems to arrive without fail, in and around your period time. When pregnant, this bloating may be a touch sooner than you'd normally expect, and more severe.

Regardless, it'll be *different* enough to make you wonder if you really are pregnant. Your hormonal changes will cause digestion processes to slow down, which also triggers bloating.

*Bowel Changes

If you're indeed pregnant, your hormones will slow, and could cause constipation. Add to that, the extra iron in your prenatal vitamin, and you could get a tad bit uncomfortable.

Make sure you drink lots of water, and eat plenty of fresh fruits and veggies, and you'll fix this minor annoyance.

Keep in mind pregnancy affects all women differently. You may end up with loose bowel movements just because. The idea is, if you see a noticeable change from the norm with your bowels, it could be an early pregnancy sign.

*Headaches

Whether it's mild, moderate, or severe headache/TMJ pain, there's nothing fun about it. Although many women don't get head pain during pregnancy, some women aren't so lucky.

The headaches in early pregnancy are linked to hormonal fluctuation, and increased blood volume. Often it's the increases in estrogen and progesterone that are to blame.

American Pregnancy states other triggers of headaches during pregnancy are:

-Sleep deprivation

-Low blood sugar levels

-Stress

-Dehydration

-Caffeine withdrawal

CIP - Cathy's Important Point - Headaches in you third trimester can result from a serious high blood pressure issues called preeclampsia. Make sure you see your doctor immediately if this is your circumstance.

*Aching Back

An aching back isn't just for the end of pregnancy. Muscle and ligaments are softening in preparation for the growth of your baby, and this can trigger back pain. Experts also note that bloating, bowel issues, and implantation cramping, may also bother your back.

*Implantation Spotting

About 20% of women experience implantation spotting in early pregnancy. It's usually described as very light, and brown, pink or red in color. It happens about a week before your period is due.

Again, this is another unusual symptom that triggers you to stop and ponder.

*Increased Temperature

If you're charting your temperatures, you'll notice a rise in temperature right after ovulation. If you've conceived, your temperatures stay elevated until your expected period.

About 7 days after ovulation, you may see another rise, a tri-phasic rise, which can be a signal you're pregnant.

Fertility Friend states it's the corpus luteum that produces the heat-inducing hormone, progesterone. This hormone gets your uterine lining ready for implantation, and causes your body temperature to rise after ovulation. The rise is typically just .4 degrees Fahrenheit, or .2 degrees Celsius.

When pregnant, your temperature will continue to rise and then level off.

If you aren't pregnant, your temperature will drop off suddenly about 10 - 16 after the temperature elevation. This triggers your monthly friend to arrive.

*Taste/Smell Changes

Maybe you love garlic, and suddenly it makes you run to the bathroom. Or perhaps you feel suddenly queasy at the smell of perfume. Your sensitivities in general change when you're pregnant, so you may be in for some unexpected surprises.

Signals you could be pregnant!

*Metallic Taste

This one's a little hard to describe, but I'll give it a shot. It's when you get this weird taste in your mouth that isn't pleasant. It's just *different*. To me it's kind of like you wiped your tongue off with a wet-wipe, or something that makes your mouth dry and weirdly flavored. It's just yucky and definitely unusual.

*Discharge

Typically right after ovulation, your cervical mucus dries up. But if you've conceived, you'll secrete more thick whitish discharge, cuz of increased estrogen levels.

Your body's already preparing to form your mucous plug. That's what needs to be dislodged down the road, in order for you to have your baby. The number one sign labor has begun.

*Moody

Many women have mood swings close to their period, cuz of hormone fluctuation. Many women report emotion with tears in early pregnancy, something noticeably different from their norm.

NOTE: You want to take note of what's atypical for you. If you're usually an emotional basket-case, then mood swings may not be an indicator you've conceived. You know yourself. Changes from your normal are what you're looking for.

*Increased Bathroom Breaks

Some women report almost immediately having to go pee a lot more than normal. Again, this makes sense, cuz your blood volume is rapidly increasing, along with the rest of the fluids in your body.

Keep in mind there are hundreds of different signs, signals, and symptoms, that *could* be your body signaling you've hit the jackpot!

Every woman is different, and so are her symptoms. All you need to do is be aware of any obvious changes in you, if you're trying to get pregnant.

One day it **WILL** add up, to a baby on its way.

Let's have a look into the pregnancy testing itself.

Pregnancy Testing

Research shows, you really should wait until you miss your period before testing. Even when there are oodles of tests claiming accurate results *up to five days sooner.* This is all dependent on how accurate your dates are, how much HCG (pregnancy hormone) you have in your system, when you test during the day, and how much liquid you've got in your bladder.

The 2 main tests are: *Home Pregnancy Tests and Blood Testing.*

Home Pregnancy Tests

There are home pregnancy tests where you pee in a cup, and others where you pee on a stick. The majority of women pee on a stick. Where you either see a plus or a negative sign, or one line is darker than the other, indicating pregnancy or not.

If you see a minus sign, or faint second line, you're not pregnant.

The problem with some of this testing, is that it's subjective. You maybe aren't quite sure if the line is darker or not. You also run the risk of getting a false negative, because every woman is different.

Essentially these tests measure the level of HCG, or pregnancy hormone, in your urine. This is an indicator of pregnancy. One thing to keep in mind, is if you get a negative result and tested early, wait a week and test again. Sometimes there just isn't enough of the hormone in your system yet.

HCG only starts appearing after the embryo has implanted in your uterine lining, and the levels continuously rise every day. You may test one day and get a faint line, and the next day it may be darker.

About a week after ovulation is the earliest your body can release a measurable amount of HCG. Just cuz it takes time for the ovum to travel down your Fallopian tubes, get fertilized, and implant firmly in your endometrial lining.

It's smart to wait at least **TEN** days after ovulation to test, as these tests really aren't cheap. If you aren't keeping track of your ovulation, test a week after your expected period.

Blood Test

In general, blood tests for pregnancy are more accurate than urine tests. Although they aren't necessarily more sensitive. During pregnancy, the human chorionic gonadotropin levels are expected to increase gradually over time, from a base level of 11, to 97 mu/ml.

Sometimes when a pregnancy is in question, repeated blood tests are done throughout the first trimester, to ensure the embryo is growing as expected.

When done correctly, a home pregnancy test is 97% accurate, but a blood test is more accurate.

A *quantitative* blood test measures the exact amount of HCG in your blood, even the smallest amounts. A *qualitative* blood test just give a yes or no answer.

Again, you should wait until at least the day you're expecting your period before testing. There are tests enabling you to find out sooner, but these tests can also be misleading in their results, because it really is too soon to tell for some.

If you can't hold yourself back, test early and get a negative, wait a week and test again just to be sure. Of course if your friend visits, that usually means you aren't pregnant.

Bright Light - In rare cases, women still get bleeding just like their period, and they're indeed pregnant. That's the exception to the rule, and not the rule though.

My Thoughts . . .

This is an incredibly exciting time, waiting to find out if you're soon going to be a mom or not. Relax and enjoy, and don't get too stressed out about it.

I highly recommend keeping a daily journal recording your feelings, thoughts, and symptoms. This'll come in helpful to have to look back upon. It's also an important tool when you're speaking with your doctor.

And as for the testing, try and hold off until a few days passed your expected period. This'll save you money on testing and retesting, and it won't cause unnecessary emotional stress on you.

A Dad-to-be's Role

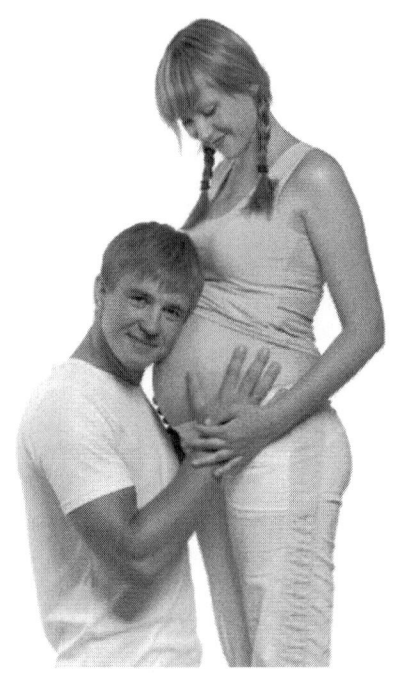

I hate to break it to you dad, but your partner is the star of this show, and rightfully so. It's her body that's going to be literally re-shaped. And she's the one that gets to ride on the roller coaster of *hormonal-triggered* emotions.

This doesn't mean she doesn't need you, because she does. She needs you to support her **ALL** the time. When she's moody, get her what she wants. If she is afraid, re-assure her. When she feels defeated, make sure you're there to show her the positive. She needs **you** to remind her you love her, and that she really isn't crazy.

There will be lots of things you *just don't understand*, and that's okay. There will be situations where you feel completely left out and even useless - that's okay too. Hang in there, and understand very soon you're going to have a beautiful new baby to help care for. And it's **your** job to help your partner get through this pregnancy process as smoothly and stress-free as possible.

If this means cleaning the house while she takes a nap - do it! If it means running to the corner store at 2 am because she has a craving for ice-cream - just do it. Anything and everything you can do to support her, is the expectation you should have of yourself right now.

Wise Advice

Sure, you're spared the morning sickness, forced weight gain, swollen ankles, achy back, and all the other physical discomforts of pregnancy, but you're in for a real shock.

It's not about how fascinated you'll be with your wife through this process. Or how touched you'll be at the helplessness of your child, or how much they need you to thrive.

But the emotional and psychological stresses a soon-to-be father faces, are often underestimated. You're worried about how good of a father you'll be. A soon-to-be-dad wonders if he'll be able to successfully support the mother and child, and if his partner will ever want to have sex again.

The issue is, most men have trouble talking about all these things.

FACT - You'll have to deal with feeling left out from day one. You don't get that physical connection your partner does with the baby growing inside of her. The baby shower isn't for the dad. Nor are all the physical symptoms that go hand in hand with being pregnant.

And after the baby is born, you'll feel a little shafted. This may pose problems, cuz nobody likes to feel left out.

CIP - Cathy's Important Pointer - It's important for you to express your feelings and get over them, for the most part anyway. It's true, the baby wants mom after birth, and why wouldn't they?

Your child has been soothed to sleep by the beat of mom's heart for almost nine months. Your baby recognizes her voice, and feels comfort in her touch. The mother also supplies the warm nourishment the baby desires around the clock, to grow and develop. The mother is all the baby knows right now. But that doesn't mean you won't get your chance to bond. That begins long before your beautiful baby enters the world.

What Can Dad Do?

You can hold your baby while mom is napping, and help change and bath him or her. Doing so strengthens the bond with your child and partner. So sure, you may need to muster up some patience, and zip your lips from time to time. But one thing for certain is, that it's all worth it the first time you hold your bundle of joy in your arms - simply amazing.

My Thoughts . . .

Sure the father may feel left out here and there, that's normal. But it's not healthy to ignore these feelings. It's important to address them, so your partner can reassure you that you're appreciated and NEEDED.

Open Communication is key.

It's perfectly normal for the father-to-be is going to be worrying too. You both need to reassure each other. Dad may not have the starring role, but that doesn't mean he's not important.

Dad...Hang in there. You're about to witness your magnificent miracle.

All three of you are important.

Now that you're Pregnant

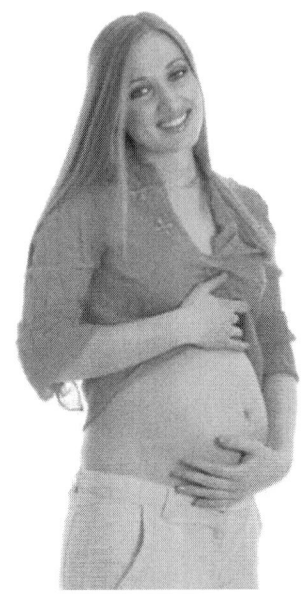

Okay, you're pregnant! Now what?

So you've confirmed you're pregnant. Here are a few things you need to take care of, in order to get prepared for your 9 month wild ride.

Schedule an appointment with your doctor or mid-wife

It's important for your mind as much as anything else, to ensure everything's on track. You need your immediate questions answered. If you've any special health condi tions, your medical provider will ease your mind, and forward the appropriate instructions.

Celebrate

Just between the two of you, have a BYOFJ (Bring Your Own Fresh Juice) party. Or perhaps a glass or two of sparkling cider to enjoy this special moment.

Some women go one step further, by planning a romantic dinner and surprising the dad. Maybe wrapping up the *pee stick* as a surprise!

Spread the Joy

By all means spread the great news to friends and family. It's important to consider waiting until you're past the first twelve weeks though. That's when most miscarriages occur. It's hard to consider and even tougher to live through. But keep in mind miscarriages are a natural process. The pregnancy is normally lost because there are problems with the developing embryo, and it's nobody's fault.

But there really is no "wrong" time to spread the news. And if you both agree - go for it!

BabyCenter suggests spreading the news whenever you're ready. It makes sense that no matter what you're going to want the love and support of your friends and family.

Educate Yourself on Pregnancy

This is why you're reading my fantabulous book!

I suggest you read any pregnancy/parenting/birthing or child development book you can get your hands on.

Follow a pregnancy calendar that tells you what's happening each day of your pregnancy. You can also sign up for pregnancy classes locally. This'll give you the information you need to make important decisions throughout your pregnancy.

Knowing what to expect before it happens, relieves stress, and give you a piece of mind, both of which are only going to help.

Care for Yourself

Getting the rest you need, eating right, and exercising regularly, are a few things you should do for you throughout this pregnancy. Listen to your body, and give it what it needs.

If you need a nap in the afternoon, find a way to take one. If you find a foot massage helps with your insomnia, put your partner to work. The important thing, is you take the time you need to feel good about yourself.

Top Secret Tidbit - The little extras really do count. Don't forget it!

Make certain you have a Support System

It doesn't matter whether you can talk with your mother, best friends, or someone at the local coffee spot. It's just so critical you have people in place you're comfortable. Trusted people to act as a sounding board, to reassure you, or to answer questions big and small.

Of course your healthcare provider should be the main source for answering your *medical* related questions.

And a good habit to get into early on, is keeping a journal of how you're feeling each day. Jot down any questions that pop into your head, or specific symptoms you're experiencing.

This helps you for two reasons. The first is to relieve immediate stress. Out of sight, out of mind right?

If you write down your thoughts, feelings, and experiences, you can relax and get on with your day. Or get back to sleep if that's what you're doing.

The other reason is, your memory might not be so sharp now that you're pregnant. It's often difficult to remember specific details when you aren't *in the moment*. Experts agree, it really doesn't take much to forget when pregnant. Or for things to get foggy fast.

Helen Christensen, PhD, says there is such a thing as *pregnancy brain,* or *momnesia*. And there are research studies showing deficits in the memory of pregnant women. Although the debate rages on, to what degree.

You can help yourself by getting into the habit of writing things down. That's only going to help.

Your life's going to change unbelievably in the next 9 months. Getting emotional is going to become the norm for you, and rightly so. Your body is changing so quickly.

How can you possibly know what to expect?

You might find yourself crying if you drop your glass of milk. Or getting angry when your partner forgets to butter your toast.

Relax, because this is all normal.

One minute you might be happy and in control. The next you may feel as if you're juggling ten tennis balls, and dropping each one. Understand this is perfectly normal. And having people you trust to talk to, helps provide the reassurance you need that you're not *crazy*.

Your hormones might be, but you aren't!

Schedule Time for the Two of you

Your relationship will go through tremendous changes. It's important to stay connected with your partner throughout. This is as simple as scheduling a weekly *date* night, where just the two of you have a nice dinner and talk.
A time for open discussions about how you're feeling, and what you're thinking. The same for your partner.

If you actually schedule these times, life won't *get in the way*. You need your partner, and your partner needs you. Commit to stay connected.

My Thoughts . . .

Trust me on this one. You need to make a little time to just enjoy the moment. It only happens once, and pretty soon you're going to be so busy with your little one, there won't be very much time to stop and smell the roses.

It's also important to let your loved ones in on the good news, but only when you're comfortable. The only people

43

that can decide when you tell others, are you and your partner. There's no wrong or right, just whenever you're ready.

Making sure you address these few pointers, helps pre-pare you mentally, physically, and emotionally, for the next fantabulous few months of your lives.

The Basics on Tests and Procedures

It's important to understand, that you don't get all caught up with the negatives of what some of these standard tests could reveal. Many of them don't give black and white answers. Taking some of them, depending on your tolerances, may cause more stress than they're worth.

There are those couples that decide they don't want any testing, and that's perfectly fine. On the other hand, oodles of couples need reassurance their baby is developing normally, and that's perfectly fine too.

On that note, here are a few of the basic tests and procedures offered when pregnant.

First Trimester Screening

First trimester screening is both fetal ultrasound and maternal blood testing, that's executed during your first three months of pregnancy, or first twelve weeks.

NT or ultrasound test for fetal nuchal translucency

This ultrasound test measures the back of the fetal neck for increased fluid, or a large diameter. Abnormal results may indicate conditions like Down syndrome or Trisomy.

Two blood maternal serum tests

These blood tests simply measure two specific substances in the blood of all expecting women.

PAPP-A or Pregnancy-Associated Plasma Protein - which is simply a protein your placenta produces in early pregnancy. If your levels are high, there's an increased risk of chromosomal issues.

HCG or Human Chorionic Gonadotropin - which is better known as the pregnancy hormone. If you're levels are too high, there is also a risk forchromosomal abnormalities.

Combined, these two tests help determine the chances of having a baby with serious chromosomal abnormalities, namely; trisomy 18 or 13, or Down syndrome.

If your results come back abnormal, you can choose whether or not you'd like further testing.

This would come in the form of:

Chorionic villus sampling - this is when a sample of the placental tissue is used to test and see with more accuracy, if there are chromosomal abnormalities with your fetus. This is usually done with a FISH or PCR, and normally takes place between 10-12 weeks of gestation.

Amniocentesis - this is performed to determine abnormalities in the fetus and infections. A small amount of amniotic fluid is drawn using a needle that's inserted through the abdomen.

It can also be used to determine the maturity of the lungs, if a baby was going to be delivered early. It's 100% accurate in determining the sex of the fetus. There's a slightly increased risk of miscarriage with this procedure. So the risks need to be weighed carefully before it's done.

Second Trimester Screening

During your second trimester of pregnancy, prenatal screening may include numerous blood tests, referred to as multiply markers. What these tests do, is determine the risk of having a baby with specific genetic conditions or birth defects. The screenings are usually performed between the 15th and 20th weeks of pregnancy.

Alpha-Fetoprotein screening or AFP - which is a blood test measuring the amount of AFP in the blood during pregnancy. This protein is usually made by the fetal liver. It's found in the amniotic fluid surrounding the fetus, and transfers into the mother's blood. Some doctors call it a maternal serum AFP.

If you have abnormal results it could mean:

47

*A neural tube defect
*Down syndrome
*Abdominal wall defects
*More than one fetus
*A due date miscalculation

Abnormal results usually indicate further testing is need-ed. It's important to understand, multiple marker screening is not completely accurate. In other words, it's giving you *the odds of,* not necessarily *what is.*

This test can cause a whole lot of stress for no reason. Or it can bring attention to a serious issue with the baby.

If a woman has this test done in the first and second tri-mester, it's more accurate.

Fetal Ultrasound

A fetal ultrasound is a great diagnostic tool to ensure your baby's doing just fine. It's a non-invasive route to see your baby before it's born. You can even get pic-tures!

Specifically, it creates an image of the fetus while still in the womb. Various parts of the fetus are measured and observed. And it can be performed trans-abdominal (through the abdomen), or trans-vaginal (through the vaginal canal).

CIP - If you're having the ultrasound early on, before 10-12 weeks, a trans-vaginal ultrasound is often used. Simp-ly because there's not a lot to see yet. When dating your pregnancy this may be used.

The ultrasound uses an electronic device referred to as a transducer, to transmit sound waves, which take readings of the baby. When the transducer is moved across the abdomen, the bouncing sound waves show up as an image. Clear jelly is placed on the device and the abdomen for smooth movement.

To give you peace of mind, fetal abnormalities are relatively uncommon, and are dependent on the age of the mother, genetics, environmental, and lifestyle factors.

These are the fetal structures looked at during an ultrasound:

*Brain and Head
*Stomach and Abdomen
*Heart
*Bladder
*Spine
*Kidneys
*Umbilical Cord
*Other specific structures

An ultrasound is low risk, and many women opt to have one around 18-20 weeks gestation, just to be certain everything's on track. This is definitely an exciting time for both mom and dad-to-be.

There are numerous other tests that may or may not be performed throughout pregnancy. This is dependent on the wishes of the parent's, and the findings of any specific test.

My Thoughts . . .

Prenatal testing can be both exciting and scary. It really is something you need to discuss with your partner and healthcare professional, to decide what you want to, and don't want to know.

Talk with your healthcare provider to learn more about your options. Don't be afraid to ask their professional for you and your baby.

Critical Care Point! *Please be reassured the majority of pregnancies go on to deliver healthy, happy bundles of joy. Sometimes knowing a little too many* what-ifs, *does more harm than good.*

*It's important to acknowledge the positive and the negative, but consciously train your mind to look for the good in everything. This makes it a little more manageable when things don't go your way.

Months One to Three Explained

Baby Development

It's always fun to know what is happening with the little one growing in your tummy. It's all so exciting and new, something that'll get you excited more and more as each day passes.

During the first month, your fetus looks like a weird small creature with a dot for eyes. It's floating around securing in the amniotic sac, which is attached to the placenta. The placenta is what transmits nutrients from you to the growing fetus.

CIP - *Everything you eat and breathe is transferred over to your unborn miracle in minuscule amounts. So be extra cautious of everything you eat and breathe, cuz now it's not just about you.*

The throat and jaw are developing, blood cells are starting to take shape, and circulation will soon start. At the end of this first month your fetus is about the size of a grain of rice.

During the second month, ears begin to develop, arms and legs are forming, along with fingers and eyes. The neural tube is intact, the digestive system has started to form, and bone begins to replace cartilage. At this point the fetus is about an inch long and weighs just 1/3 of an ounce.

By the end of the third month, your baby is fully formed. You little one can even open and close its tiny fists. Teeth are starting to grow, reproductive organs are manifesting, and the liver even produces bile. It's really difficult to determine the sex at this point, cuz your little one is only about 3-4 inches, and only weighs an ounce.

Mom Growth and Change

By the end of the 5th week of pregnancy, a pregnancy test is fairly accurate, the uterus lining is thickening, and determining pregnancy by ultrasound testing, is doable in another week.

During the first month of pregnancy your hormones are going crazy. Breasts are tender and larger, your body feels tired, and nausea and food cravings are likely.

During the second month, you're going to feel the need to pee more often. Of course your abdomen is starting to swell, and your pants may feel snug. Your systems are working overtime, and it's important that you get the extra rest you need, eat well, and exercise regularly, in order to prepare for delivering your little miracle.

TRUTH - Some women seem to sail through pregnancy without issue.

But most experience some sort of discomfort. Dizziness, light-headedness, and mood swings are common. Your skin changes may start to appear too. Many women get a beautiful glow to their skin, and others end up with acne and irritated red skin.

Don't stress over it. Remember, it's just your body doing what it needs to for your baby.

My Thoughts . . .

This is an exciting time of growth for both mother and baby. By the end of this first trimester, your little one is actually looking human. Also, by the end of this first trimester, you should start to feel better. A little more used to all the whacky changes your body is going through.

Make sure you relax, eat well, exercise, and sleep when you can. Both you and your baby need every ounce of energy you can manifest, to grow and develop happily.

Months Four to Six Explained

Baby Development

In the second trimester of pregnancy, your baby is actually starting to resemble a baby, not an alien!

The fingers and toes are well developed, facial features are forming nicely, and your baby can even suck their thumb. The nervous system is functioning, and the reproductive organs are fully developed.

Exciting is the fact your baby's heart can be heard with a Doppler!

At the end of the fourth month, your baby is about 6 inches long, and weighs in at about 4 ounces. According to *BabyCenter* experts, the skeleton is transforming from cartilage to bone.

In the fifth month hair is starting to grow, that covers the entire body. This protects your baby from the fluids surrounding it. And the whitish coating called vernix caseosa, also helps protect the skin from the amniotic fluid.

Eyebrows and eyelids are also in place.

At the end of the fifth month your baby is almost a pound and measures in close to 10 inches in length.

And by the time you reach the end of six months, your baby is close to 12 inches long and weighs about 2 pounds. Their skin is thin and wrinkled, the eyelids begin forming, and you will feel movement a lot more.

BabyCenter specialists say this is also where the skin begins smoothing out as fat starts to accumulate.

If born early, your baby could survive after about 23 week's gestation with special care.

Mom Growth/Change

At this point in your pregnancy, you'll start to feel some light kicking and punching, a truly exciting moment. This really does make it more *real* for you. Chances are, your breasts are at least a size or two larger than usual. It's important get measured and buy a supportive bra, so you're secure and comfortable.

Note - Make a point of having a lingerie expert actually show you how to take you bust measurements. Most retail associates are happy to help. If you're shopping in a maternity shop, even better

In month 5, you may experience discomfort from the skin on your tummy stretching. Lots of moisturizing will help. Leg and back pain may also surface, depending on the path of your pregnancy. Be ready for oodles of trips to the bathroom too, as you uterus continues to grow and nudge your bladder.

In the 6th month, there's a pretty good chance you're going to have back pain, cuz your ligaments are stretched to the max, to support your enlarging uterus. If you stand too long, your legs and feet may start to swell.

Make sure you listen to your body and before it starts to hurt, rest.

My Thoughts . . .

By the end of the 6th month, your little may be described as a hairy white teeny-tiny human being. It will be fully formed in the basic terms, and continuing develop, in order transform viable outside the womb.

You'll hopefully be getting your second wind now, and really enjoy pregnancy as it unfolds. Keep taking care of yourself.

Get the rest you need, exercise daily, and choose healthy foods you need to stay strong.

It won't be long now!

Months Seven to Nine Explained

Baby Development

Time really does fly. At the end of the 7th month of pregnancy your baby really starts to store fat. The baby is now about 14 inches long, and weights 2-4 pounds. The hearing is fully developed and your baby responds to external stimuli.

Born early, after the seventh month of pregnancy, your baby has a good chance of surviving with medical assistance.

Did you know? Your little one can open and close their eyes, and probably even see!

At the end of 8 months, your baby is about 18 inches long, and weighs close to 5 pounds. It will continue to put on weight, and fine tune the senses. Lungs should be *almost* mature at this point.

Moving towards the end stretch. Your baby continues to develop rapidly. The eyes and limbs are moving regularly, and positioning changes as your baby gets set for delivery.

Your little miracle will drop down into the pelvis, with their head usually facing down. At the end of this month, the baby's normally about 18-20 inches long, and weighs in at about 7 healthy pounds.

Mom Growth/Change

By the 7th month of pregnancy, you may feel Braxton-Hicks. This is referred to as false labor. Which are just what medical specialists call warm-up contractions. Your body is practicing contractions in labor.

As long as these contractions don't merge closer together, and get stronger on the pain scale, they're perfectly normal Braxton-Hicks. If you're unsure, make sure you call your doctor.

It's better to be safe than sorry. And when you truly are in No-Mans-Land, checking is a wise-owl smart move.

60

By the end of the eighth month, you may feel drops of pre-milk or colostrum from your nipples. In addition, you could begin to feel light contractions. As well, your body's dividing the oxygen in the lungs with the baby, which explains why you're feeling out of breath so much.

You're almost there!

In the ninth month, your belly button could be sticking out, and your vagina lips will be swollen and ready. Your baby will soon be here. All you've gotta do, is wait until it decides to arrive!

My Thoughts . . .

This last trimester is tough, but definitely worth it the first time you get to hold your new little miracle. Make sure you're aware of pending labor signs, and your bag is packed and ready to go, just in case.

According to WebMD, the majority of babies aren't born on their estimated due date. So you need to be ready. It's really important to listen to your body. If you're tired, make sure you rest. And stick to eating small nutritious snacks regularly, to keep your blood sugar level, and energy steady and available.

You're just about there!

Eating Healthy for 1.1

Healthy eating during pregnancy is important for both mother and baby. What you need to keep in mind, is just because you're having a baby, doesn't mean you're eating for two!

After the first month, the other *being* inside you, is the size of a grain of rice.

How much food do you think a grain of rice needs?

That's just to bring you perspective. Yes, you need to eat more than you normally would, because your bodily systems are burning more calories and working harder. But it's not a whole lot more, just so we're clear.

So how many calories extra do you need when pregnant?

The truth is, during your first and second trimesters, you really don't need any extra calories. The average woman needs 2,000 calories a day to maintain her weight. This varies according to height and weight, body composition, health status, level of exercise, and lifestyle.

Although, if you're pregnant and between the ages of 15 and 18, you're still growing, and need an extra hundred calories a day from the start.
There is a shift during the third trimester. Energy demands on the body increase significantly, and an extra 200 calories a day is recommended

It's important to eat the *right* amount of food throughout your pregnancy, so you gain the weight that's right for you and your baby.

You may need a different amount of calories if:

*You were underweight before you got pregnant
*You were overweight before you got pregnant
*You're having more than one baby

Here are a few samples of 200 calorie snacks, that'll energize you, and help you stay strong for the final leg of your pregnancy journey:

*Two slices of whole grain bread with peanut butter

*One banana, and a cup of low-fat cottage cheese
*One cup of low-fat yogurt, and a cup of fresh fruit
*Ten whole grain crackers, and a cheese string
*One cup of pretzels, and a large orange
*Two stalks of celery with half of a tablespoon of peanut butter each, and a mango
*One cup frozen of vegetables, and half of a small whole grain bagel with a smear of jam

And just in general, you should be getting foods from the 4 main food groups daily, including:

*6-8 servings of fruits and vegetables
*4-6 servings of healthy whole grains
*2-3 servings of lean meats and meat alternates
*2-3 servings low-fat milk products

Serving Sizes

Serving sizes are often perceived to be grossly exaggerated. For instance, restaurant servings are usually 3-4 times the amount you really need.

A serving of fruit is one piece, or 3/4 of a cup chopped. A serving of vegetables is 3/4 of a cup.

A serving of healthy whole grains, is half of a whole grain bagel, or 3/4 of a cup of cooked brown rice or pasta.

For meat, it's the size of a deck of cards. If you're having eggs, it's one large egg.

With milk and milk products, one cup of milk is a serving, or 3/4 of a cup of yogurt.

Many people are truly surprised at just how much smaller portions are supposed to be, compared to their usual eating. It's all about creating new healthy eating habits, and pregnancy is a great time to start.

Here are a few healthy eating tips to help you sail through pregnancy:

Never forget to eat breakfast

The saying is true, breakfast is the most important meal of the day.

* Ready to eat or whole grain cooked breakfast cereals with fruit are good. This gives you important nutrients like iron and calcium.

* If your tummy isn't cooperating, stick with dry whole grain toast or crackers.

Get plenty of fiber

* Plenty of fresh fruits and veggies gives you the nutrients you need and the fiber required to keep waste moving through.

* Brown rice and pasta, and whole grain foods are great.

* You can't go wrong with beans of any sort.

Snack wisely

Snacking is a great way to keep up with the energy demands of your body. But it's important to note, healthy snacking is what your body needs, NOT junk food.

*Low-fat or reduced fat yogurt with fresh fruit or granola.

*Whole grain crackers with cream cheese or peanut butter.

Don't forget your prenatal vitamin

It's very important you get all the essential vitamins and minerals your body needs to support the healthy growth of your baby. A prenatal vitamin makes sure your iron levels are good, and the folic acid helps ensure your baby develops normally.

Researchers at *MayoClinic* report, if you're pregnant or trying, prenatal vitamins are essential.

*The folic acids helps prevent neural tube defects.

*The iron supports healthy growth and development of your baby.

This supplement also decreases the risk of low birth weight.

Plan to eat 2-3 meals of seafood each week

Omega fatty acids are important in the growth and development of your baby. Fish sources are best for this. So make sure you have 2-3 meals each week with fish. Research shows it's more easily absorbed than in supplement form.

*A serving is about the size of a deck of cards.

*Avoid fish with high levels of mercury, like shark, and swordfish.

*Great fish to eat are sardines, salmon, and shrimp.

Steer clear of processed luncheon meats and soft cheeses

You don't have to freak out if you happen to eat these items. It's just in your best interest to avoid them if possible, cuz they may have bacteria that's harmful to your baby.

Try not to eat:

*Feta, goat cheese, and Brie.

*Sushi or undercooked meats.

*Lunch meats or hot dogs, unless they're cooked thoroughly.

Easy on the caffeine and no alcohol

If you can make the switch to decaffeinated coffee, great. If not, try and limit yourself to 1-2 cups a day. Of course alcohol is just plain dangerous for a developing baby. So stay clear of it.

*Try and drink decaffeinated coffee or tea.

*Drink water in place of pop or soda.

*No alcohol.

My Thoughts . . .

You really need to pay attention to what you're eating and how much. If your tummy is rumbling, then eat! Just make sure you're smart about it.

Grab a peanut butter sandwich on whole grain bread and a banana, or a handful of nuts and a small yogurt. This helps you keep your weight gain steady, and gives you a peace of mind, that you are nourishing your body the best of your knowledge.

Of course the odd treat is perfectly fine. Just make some limitations for yourself. Instead of eating a whole bag of cookies, have one or two. And don't eat the whole tub of ice-cream in one sitting. Have a small bowl and put it away for next time!

Getting Prepared for Baby

Nine months to prepare for your new little bundle of joy to arrive seems like a lot, but really it's not.

Here are a few tips to get prepared for the big day.

One - Get Packed!

Pack a hospital bag early, just in case baby decides to arrive early. You'll want to pack pj's, slippers, socks, and an extra t-shirt or two. Pack a comfortable going home outfit. Probably something you wore around 6 months, and lots of undies.

You'll want to pack diapers, wipes, baby cream, and 5 or 6 sleepers for the baby, unless the hospital provides them. Bring your camera, books, journal, lip balm, cd's, and tennis balls for massaging, if you experience back labor.

Also, throw in your favorite pillow, and don't forget a going home blanket for the baby.

You'll need your regular toiletry items, mints or hard candies to suck on, and snacks for your partner.

Two - Clothing Prep

Wash all your baby items and bedding in laundry detergent designed to be extra gentle on a baby's skin. The last thing you need to worry about with a newborn, is itchy skin and painful rash that's preventable.

Three - Car Seat

Most hospitals won't let you leave with a newborn unless you have the proper car seat, and rightly so. An infant seat is something you should buy brand new. It's very important the seat hasn't ever been in a car accident. And the only way to be certain is to buy a brand new one.

Also, get it installed by the experts. If you go to the local police station or fire department there's someone that'll do it for you, and show you the tricks for doing it yourself. Just do it, cuz a car seat installed incorrectly can mean serious injury or death.

According to *American Academy of Pediatrics*, it's recommended ALL hospitals set policies requiring every newborn leaves the hospital in a safe car seat.

Four - Find You Doctor

Do a little investigative research and figure out what pediatrician you'd like for your baby. Make certain you're both on the same page. You've got important life decisions ahead that you need to trust your child's pediatrician with.

Some people choose to just have a family doctor, the choice is yours.

Five - Child Care

If you're planning on going back to work after your maternity leave, get child care lined up now. It's not unusual for daycares to have waiting lists, and some only except infants after a certain age. Find one that you're comfortable with, can afford, and that's got space when you need it.

Six - Birthing Prep

Make sure you go to birthing classes with your partner. This helps ease some of your anxiety about having the baby. It also gets you comfortable with the venue of where you're planning on delivering.

If you're planning a home birth, childbirth classes are still beneficial.

The unknown is the scary part!

Seven - Pre-Registration

If you're giving birth in a hospital, ensure you're pre-registered. Always have your list of emergency contacts in your purse and with your partner, just in case you go into labor early.

The last thing you need, is fumbling around with phone numbers when you're having contractions!

My Thoughts . . .

Having a baby is both and exciting and nerve racking for the both of you. It's important to prepare sooner, just in case you do happen to go into labor early. Emotion and logic just doesn't mix!

Prepare and give yourself the peace of mind you deserve!

Types of Delivery and Mindset

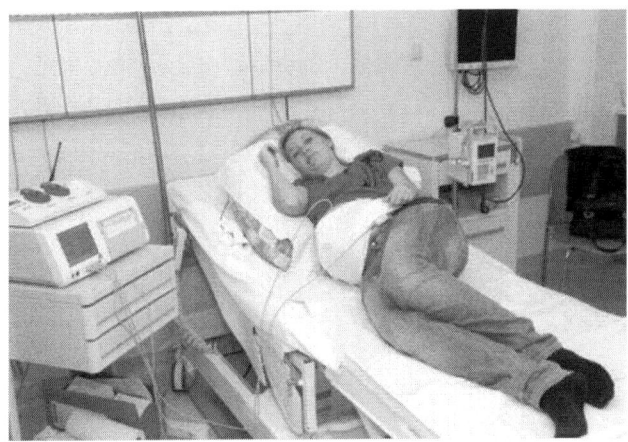

Please keep an open mind, because there are times when you can't choose how, or when, you'll deliver your baby.

Bottom line is, your baby needs to be delivered safely, and you need to fare well through the process.

Healthy and happy is the focus here.

There are different kinds of childbirth for different reasons.

There are three main types:

Natural

Medicated

*Cesarean

Natural

This delivery is without pain medication. Whether your child arrives naturally in the hospital or at home, or in the back of your car on the way to the hospital without medication, it's a natural birth.

There are many naturalistic programs that teach women how to control their pain with their mind naturally. This prepares you mentally, to give birth without any medical intervention.

Women report this is often extremely rewarding, but it can also be traumatic, and extremely painful if you aren't mentally prepared.

Medicated Birth

There are many women out there that are terrified at the thought of delivering naturally, and that's okay. Some women prefer to use some sort of medication to reduce some of the pain of delivering naturally.

If you plan on a natural delivery with medication, ensure your doctor knows beforehand, so you understand your options. Remember if your labor progresses too quickly, you might not have time to get your epidural, or pain relief of choice.

A blessing in disguise, but only after the fact!

VIP - In an emergency situation, a general anesthesia may be necessary.

Analgesics are medications used to relieve pain, and *anesthetics* are medications that give you a loss of sensation.

Examples of analgesics are aspirin and Tylenol, simple used to lessen pain. Demerol is also a strong pain reliever that may be used intravenously. Sometimes the baby has trouble breathing immediately after birth when analgesics are used.

How do they work?

Anesthetics interrupt the pathway of nerves that takes pain sensations to your brain. Basically they *block* your pain. A doctor can opt to numb you from the waist down, or just your vaginal area during your delivery.

There are mainly anesthetic options. The epidural, pudendal, spinal and caudal are most commonly used.

Epidural

*The epidural numbs you from the waist down. It's used for both a vaginal and cesarean delivery. A long needle is inserted into the lower back, precisely into a space in your spinal cord. This is where a tube is placed, and medication is released as required. It usually takes up to 30 minutes to take full effect.

PubMedHealth, says a women that's allergic to anesthetics, or that has a rare blot clotting disorder, should not use this pain relief method to be safe.

Pudendal

*The pudendal block is given through a needle inserted into the vaginal area. This numbs that area only for the delivery.

Spinal Block

*A spinal block is used at the end of labor, right before delivering. It instantly numbs the body from the waist down. It's often used for cesarean deliveries. This sort of block can interfere with the descending of the head of the baby into the cervix, so it's not usually given during vaginal deliveries, until the cervix is totally dilated.

Caudal Block

*A caudal block is often used during labor and delivery. It's not as effective as an epidural, and may also slow the progress of labor, as larger doses are required. It's given by a long needle insertion to the lower back.

Cesarean Delivery and General Anesthesia

With general anesthesia, you're knocked completely out. This is reserved for dire emergency situations. Long ago it used to be used a little more regularly, but times have changed.

With a cesarean delivery, some are done for medical reasons and others are optional. This method of delivery is when your child is delivered through a small incision in your abdomen and uterus. It's considered major surgery, and comes with risks and potential complications.

The good news is, many babies delivered through cesarean wouldn't have survived a vaginal birth.

A few reasons for a C-section delivery are:

* Failure to progress in labor
* A very large baby
* The baby is breech
* A premature deliver
* Previous C-section delivery

Note to dads: *If your partner ends up delivering by C-section, she needs your support more than ever. Reassure her constantly. Tell her she did a great job, and this best for her and the baby. Also set up help around the house for cleaning, groceries, and food preparation to start. Often hiring a housekeeper for a short time is a great investment if it's affordable.*

My Thoughts . . .

It's important to inform yourself about your birthing options, and discuss with your medical provider what's best for you. Keep your mind open, cuz you won't always have your choice of delivery.

The best choice is the one safest for both yourself and your precious little miracle.

Make a plan, and more often than not everything will turn out just fine.

The Delivery and Shortly After

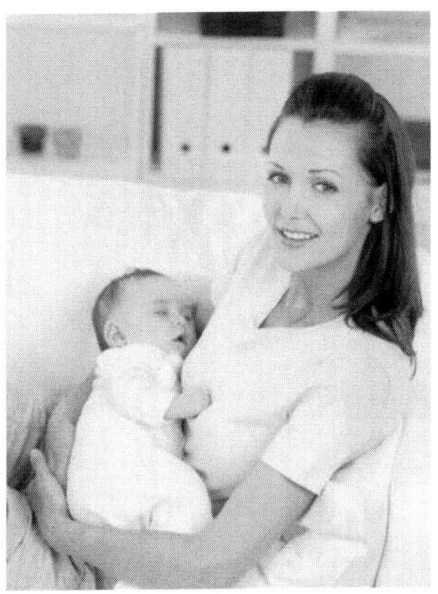

After your bundle of joy is delivered, emotions and hor-mones will be running wild. Get as much rest as possible, and accept help around the house and with the baby when you can.

It takes time for your body to recover, whether you've had a vaginal or surgical delivery.

If you delivered naturally, you'll be sore for at least a few weeks. Take it slow and easy, and soon you'll be feeling a whole lot better. If you tore during delivery, take it even slower.

Most women report the second or third day after the delivery is the toughest. Each day after gets a little easier.

If you've delivered by cesarean, you're going to need quite a bit longer to recover. Your doctor will give you explicit instructions to follow. Normally you'll need to wait four to six weeks to do any sort of lifting, other than your baby.

You'll also need help around the house for at least a few weeks. It's important to rest and help with the baby, so you'll recover quicker. This enables you to take wonderful care of your new little one.

If you are choosing to breastfeed, you may need some professional help. Unknown to many, breastfeeding is **not** natural for a baby, it's learned. The technique anyway.

It's smart to have a lactation consultant help you with it from the start, to prevent problems. There's nothing fun about having sore and bleeding nipples!

Here are a few other things to be wary of after delivering.

*Crowd Control

This one's for the partner. It's your responsibility to make sure mom and baby aren't overwhelmed with too many visitors. I know this can be tough with family members, but they're going to have to understand you need time to bond as a family, and your partner needs rest, as does your little one.

The best option is to have friends and family come to visit in the hospital, then limit the visitors for the next few weeks. This allows time for recovery, and getting used to your new baby

*Let People Help

If someone offers to help, take them up on it. Have them make meals for a week to put in your freezer, or run to the grocery store for you. Maybe you need them to do some errands. Regardless, if people offer to help, let them.

*Mood Swings

You may find yourself exhausted one minute and elated the next. This is perfectly normal. Your hormones are working their way back to *normal* after delivery, and they're taking the long route.

You may be feeling *fat,* and might be snapping at your partner more than normal. Give yourself a break. Your body has just gone through some extremely trying changes, and you should be proud.

Things WILL get better!

*Milk is coming

Get ready for your milk to come in. Usually between 2 and 5 days after birth, according to *Dr. Jan Moreau,* MD. This is extremely uncomfortable initially, as your breasts become painful and rock hard, until you little one drinks.

The message here is to persevere. Feed your baby often to relieve your breasts, and to encourage a good milk supply to develop.

Most experts recommend feeding at least every 4 hours until your milk supply is well established. If this isn't your first pregnancy, then you may be able to get away with stretching this out a little, cuz believe it or not, your breasts do remember.

Mine remembered SIX times! lol

If you've delivered a larger baby, supplementing may be necessary initially, because your breasts can't supply your baby all the calories it requires just yet. Don't despair, cuz before you know it, your breasts will be up for the challenge.

*Eat Well - Drink a Lot

It's very important you continue to eat healthy and often after delivery, to keep your energy up. You'll also need to drink a lot, in order to get your milk production up. If you're breast feeding, eat an extra 2-300 calories per day.

This equates to a banana, a cup of yogurt, and 10 almonds, or half of a bagel with peanut butter, and a glass of skim milk.

You should also be drinking water before, during, and after feedings. The last thing you want is get dehydrated. That negatively affects milk production.

*Expect Bleeding

You'll bleed after delivery for at least the next few weeks. It'll start off bright red and heavy, and gradually get lighter, and turn pink or brown, before transforming clear.

An icky nuisance. But part of the package!

CIP - If you can get your hands on some of those disposable mesh undies most hospitals carry, that's awesome! They're much easier to keep your gynormous pad in place with than a regular pair of ten dollar panties!

*Uterus

Your uterus will remain large, and your cervix won't return to its normal pre-pregnancy size until about 6 weeks after delivery. Through this process you'll continue to feel contractions, although nothing like during your delivery.

Don't fret cuz it's all normal!

*Exercising

It's advised you wait 3-4 weeks after a natural delivery to get back to your exercise routine, and about 6 weeks after a C-section. But there are breathing exercises and stretches you can perform right after delivery, that'll help get your body back faster.

Rule of Thumb - The fitter you were going into pregnancy, the faster you can get back to your normal.

*Warnings

If you find that you have a fever right after delivering, pass a blood clot larger than a lemon, or have extremely heavy bleeding that won't let up, you need to call your doctor.

As well, if you have a smelly vaginal discharge, or very painful spots on your breasts that are hot to touch, call your doctor. The latter could be blocked milk ducts or what's called mastitis. Sometimes massaging these hard lumps in your breasts helps, but beware it's very painful.

A few other reasons to call your doctor, are if you're having trouble going pee, if it's painful, or if you've tenderness and pain in your legs.

It's just better to be safe than sorry.

My Thoughts . . .

Having a baby is such a gynormously wonderful learning experience. Keep in mind lots of changes are taking place, and there will be sleepless nights and annoying symptoms to deal with.

That's just part of the process.

Try to relax, keep a positive attitude, get as much rest as you can, eat healthy, and exercise when able. You'll be surprised how quickly time flies by. What's also important, is taking time out for you each day. Even if it's just having your partner watch the baby for a couple hours while you get a nap in.

Your health, both mentally and physically, is important for the happiness for you, your baby, and your partner.

Final Thoughts . . .

The miracle of birth never ceases to amaze me. How a tiny zygote can grow and develop into a baby in just 9 months is mind-blowing. Experiencing the journey emotionally and physically through to the birth is phenomenal.

It's inspiring how powerful the connective bond is between mother and child, and simply heartwarming to watch a new father light up at first sight of his new son or daughter.

It's truly a magical moment.

By understanding the processes involved in pregnancy and delivery, you're arming yourself with the information required to make your pregnancy run a smooth as silk.

There will be bumps in the road. And by preparing yourself early, you're always be headed positively in the right direction.

Good luck to you, and make sure you take the time to stop and enjoy what a truly special miracle the birth of your child is!

Last Thoughts…

*THANK-YOU for reading my masterpiece. I hope you learned a little something, or at least got a few smiles.
*I would appreciate a millisecond or three of your time for a quick review, to help me build my masterful book empire higher.
*Whatever you do, don't forget to smile, and of course, check out my website for more of my e-Book masterpieces at: www.flawlesscreativewriting.com

Cathy☺

Printed in Great Britain
by Amazon.co.uk, Ltd.,
Marston Gate.